TRANSPORTATION:
Then *and* NOW

Contents

Rigby.

Introduction

Look in the streets, by the shore, and in the sky. What do you see? You probably see many ways that people move around: bicycles, trains, ships, cars, and planes. People used to walk everywhere, but then they thought of a few new ways to move around.

Bicycles

Can you imagine riding a bicycle without pedals? Long ago there was a wooden bicycle that the rider moved by pushing his feet on the ground.

1817 The hobby horse was invented.

1800   1850

Another bicycle of long ago had a metal frame, wooden wheels, and a front wheel that was taller than you! This bicycle was called the bone shaker. It was very uncomfortable!

1870 The high-wheeler was invented.

1900

Today's bicycles are not as heavy, clumsy, and uncomfortable as the old ones. There are bicycles for racing, for mountain biking, or for just having fun.

1984 Bicyclists prepared for the Summer Olympic Games.

1950

Each type of bike may look different, but they all have the same basic parts that were developed more than 100 years ago: a seat, handlebars, pedals, and brakes.

2001 World Mountain Bike Championships junior downhill races took place.

brakes

handlebars

2000

pedals

Trains

Did you know trains once ran on wooden tracks and were pulled by animals or even people?

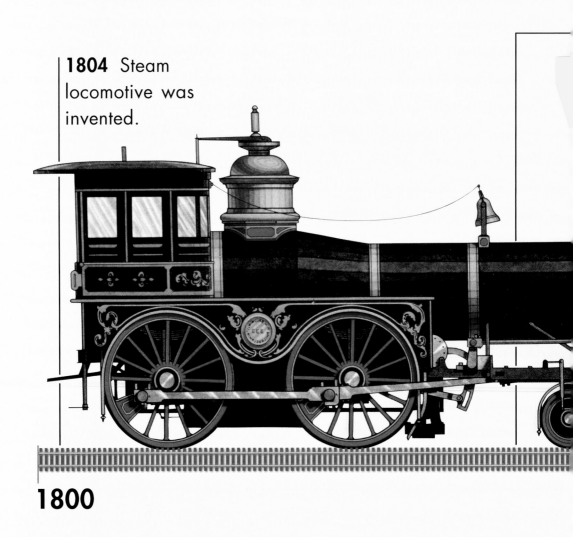

1804 Steam locomotive was invented.

1800

In the 1800s, steam-powered locomotives pulled the first trains. The steam train moved so fast that some people were afraid of them. At that time, a train could go about 20 miles per hour.

1830 A famous race was held between a horse and a steam locomotive.

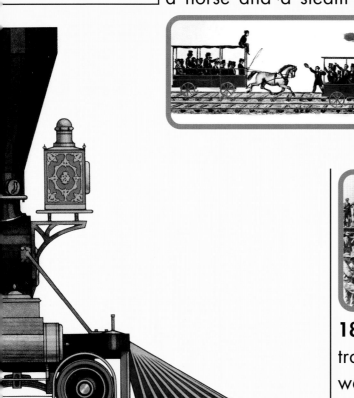

1869 First transcontinental railroad was completed.

1850

Over time trains became faster and more comfortable. Some cities even built underground train systems called subways.

1897 Boston became the first U.S. city to have a subway.

1900

Improvements are still being made.
Maglev trains move as they actually
float above a magnetic track. These trains
can zoom along at speeds up to 300 miles
per hour.

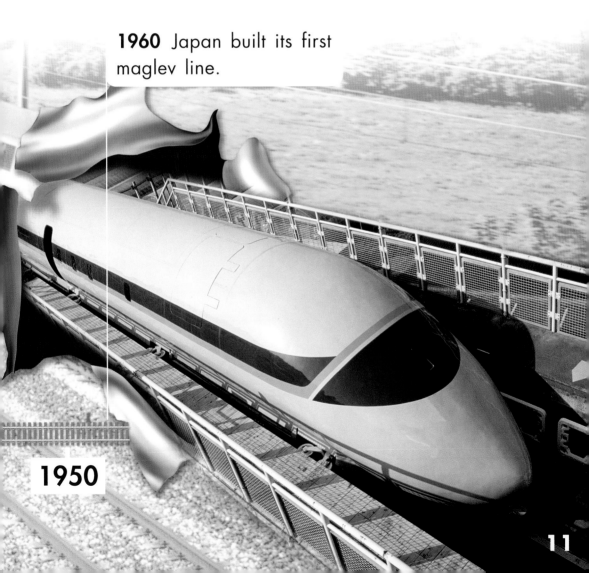

1960 Japan built its first
maglev line.

1950

Ships

Have you ever wondered how people traveled by water long ago? Originally people traveled in simple canoes.

300 The Maya lived in Tulum, where they used canoes to transport goods.

793 The first recorded Viking raids occurred in Britain.

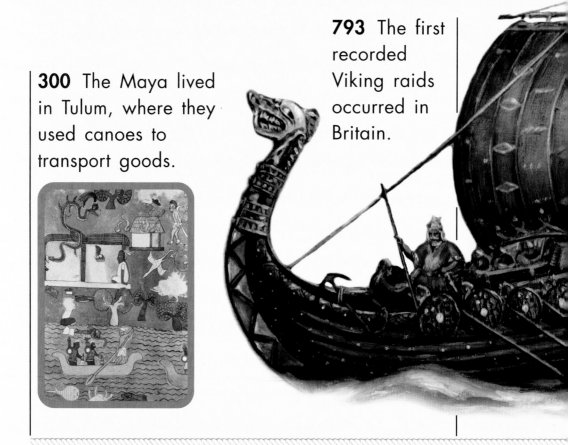

500

Then large boats  required many men to row. Ships that needed sails came later. Now when we look at the ships of long ago, we wonder how they ever sailed.

1450 Full-rigged sailing ship was developed.

1000

Water travel really changed when people began using steam-powered ships to take long trips.

WHITE STAR LINE.

"OLYMPIC". 45,000 TONS. AND "TITANIC". 45,000 TONS.

THE LARGEST STEAMERS IN THE WORLD.

1912 The steam-powered Titanic struck an iceberg and sank in the North Atlantic Ocean.

1500

Today's ships are very advanced. Diesel
and gas engines power more modern ships,
and many use a special kind of energy
called nuclear power.

2000 Many U.S.
combat warships are
nuclear powered.

2000

Cars

Can you imagine riding in a car with only three wheels? At the end of the 19th century, the first automobile looked quite different. It didn't have a roof or windshield, and it only had three wheels.

1885 Karl Benz built a successful gasoline engine.

1880   1900

Early cars were very expensive because they were made by hand. Then someone had the idea to use an assembly line to put cars together, and they became much more affordable.

1908
Henry Ford introduced the Model T automobile.

1914 Henry Ford established the first moving assembly line.

1920

Many new vehicles have resulted from the invention of the car. Specialized vehicles now serve different purposes:

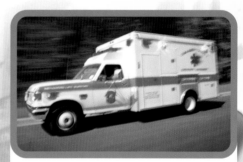

1997 An ambulance helped to save Detroit Lions' football player Reggie Brown.

1950s Red double-decker buses were popular in London.

1940

1960

- Buses for public transportation
- Ambulances for taking people to the hospital
- Fire trucks for fighting fires

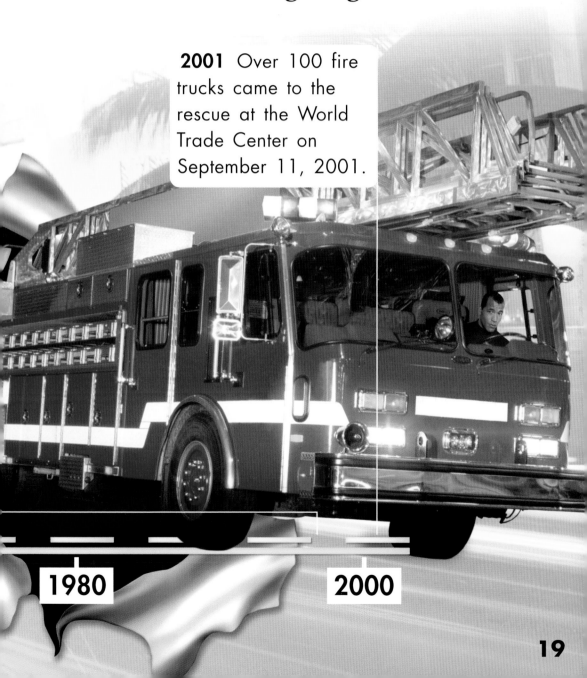

2001 Over 100 fire trucks came to the rescue at the World Trade Center on September 11, 2001.

1980

2000

Airplanes

Have you ever wanted to fly? Some people have always had the desire to soar above the clouds. The first flights were in hot-air balloons and gliders. It is believed people in ancient times tried to build kites strong enough to lift a person.

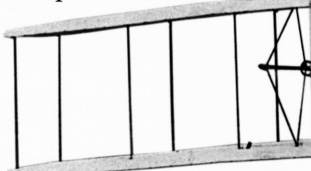

1783 First hot-air balloon flight.

1800

1850

Eventually in 1903 two brothers made an airplane that stayed in the air for 12 seconds. That airplane didn't look like the planes we have today, but it made us believe that flying was possible.

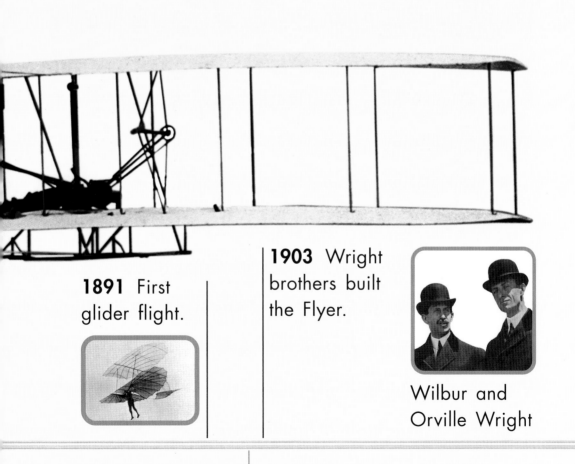

1891 First glider flight.

1903 Wright brothers built the Flyer.

Wilbur and Orville Wright

1900

Flying is the fastest way to travel these days. In fact, some airplanes can fly faster than the speed of sound!

1937 Amelia Earhart attempted to fly around the world.

1969 The Concorde made its first test flight.

1950

Whether you choose to travel by plane, train, ship, or bicycle, one thing is for sure—there are plenty of different ways to get around!

1981 The first space shuttle blasted off.

2000

Glossary

assembly line – a row of machines and people working together to make a product

diesel engine – an engine that uses diesel fuel to make it go

glider – an aircraft without an engine

locomotive – the train engine that pushes or pulls a train

Index